Learn HTML in 1 Hour For Beginners

By Jasdeep Khalsa

Learn HTML in 1 Hour For Beginners
By Jasdeep H. B. S. Khalsa

ISBN-13: 9798645905781

Contents

Introduction

Learn to make your own websites in 1 hour from now, starting from scratch.

Let's get started right away as we now only have 59 minutes left!

Who is this for?

If you're looking to:

- Build a website from scratch
- Edit an existing website or HTML template

Then congratulations, you're in the right place.

What you need to get started

There are just a few simple things you need to get started:

1. A **computer** with a large screen e.g. a laptop or desktop. Keep this beside you as you read through so you can try out the examples as the best way to learn website development is by doing it.

2. An **internet connection** - it doesn't have to be fast but a stable connection is ideal

3. A **modern web browser** like Google Chrome, Firefox or Edge

If in doubt, download and install Google Chrome by going here: Google.com/chrome

The 3 Pillars of the Web

There are **three** main **computer languages** which power the whole Internet and every website you will ever visit or build.

These are:

1. **HTML** – This language is for providing **structure** & **content** to a page, but leaves the page looking **unstyled** and honestly quite ugly looking e.g. imagine text, form fields, images, audio & video on a page but all unstyled.

2. **CSS** – This provides **design** & **style** to the page and makes it look beautiful. It can also give a page some basic animations.

3. **JavaScript** – Finally, this is the more complex of the three languages and provides **interactivity** to a page, for example complex animations, submitting a form or sending & receiving information from other websites & apps.

Please note: JavaScript is **not** the same as Java, even though they share a long history together!

In this book we're focussing on the first and arguably the most important language of the web: **HTML**.

But don't sweat it, we'll cover **CSS** & **JavaScript** too in my upcoming books at JasdeepKhalsa.com/books.

The Three Pillars of the Web - HTML, CSS & JavaScript

An Awesome Online Code Editor

Throughout this book we'll be using the excellent online editor:

Glitch.com

It's an online code editor on which we can create everything from basic web pages to complex web apps.

Practical
- Go to Glitch.com
- Click the **New Project** button and the **hello-webpage** project
- Have a poke around and get familiar with the options available in this code editor

---

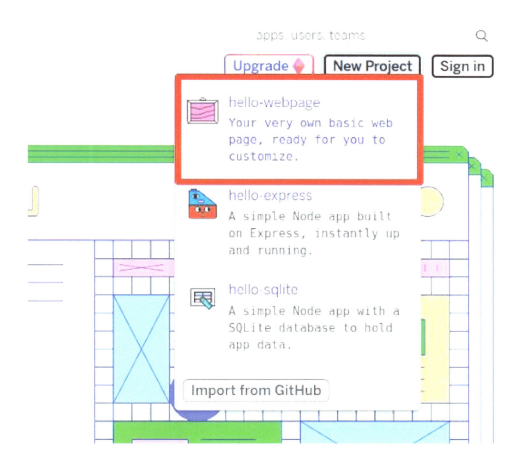

Glitch.com homepage showing various projects which can be setup. For now we're interested in the hello-webpage project

4 Language Rules of HTML

The entire language of HTML can be summarised in **four simple rules**:

1. **<p>** - **Start of a tag** e.g. paragraph

As soon as you see the less than (**<**) and more than (**>**) brackets, you know this is the **beginning** of a new page **structure** or **content** tag.

2. **</p>** - **End of a tag** e.g. paragraph

As soon as you see the less than with a slash (**</**) and more than (**>**) brackets, you know this is the **end** of a new page **structure** or **content** tag, which must have **started somewhere earlier in the page**.

3. **<img />** – A **self-closing tag** (does not need an end tag) e.g. image

This is a special case, in that some tags are allowed to close themselves. So this is both the **beginning** and **end** of this tag in one go. We'll cover in detail later which tags this applies to.

4. <img **src="dog.jpg"** /> – An **attribute** added to the image tag which has a **value** of "dog.jpg". Attributes change the behaviour of the tag in some way e.g. this shows the image dog.jpg on the page

Finally, it's important to know that any given **structure** or **content** tag can contain a number of **specific attributes** and **values** which go into those attributes.

There are also a number of **generic attributes** and **values** that apply to all tags e.g. *id*, *class*.

Normally we don't try to remember all of these tags, attributes or values in our head, instead we use a reference to help us, like my favourite one **W3Schools**:

W3Schools.com/tags

Basic Structure of a HTML Page

Every webpage on a website has a common structure:

<!DOCTYPE html> - A special tag which tells the browser what version of HTML to render the page with. The tag shown is the **latest** & **recommended** version.

<html> - Start of the HTML page

   <head></head> - This does not render on the page, but can help inform the browser or search engines what the page contains and can include files which should be loaded with the page e.g. styles written in CSS or scripts written in JavaScript

   <body></body> - This renders content or HTML tags on the page

</html> - End of the HTML page

That was not too difficult, right?

Remember, **every** website or webpage on the Internet follows this exact same structure, so now that you know this format you can understand any website's structure easily.

Now for a bit of a practical.

Practical
- Go back to Glitch.com
- Enable the web preview using the **Show** button and read the HTML in the *index.html* file
- For any HTML tags you don't understand, look them up on W3Schools.com/tags

---

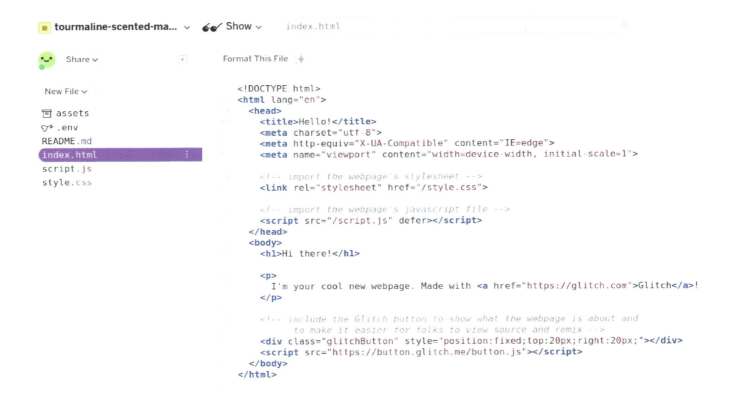

Glitch.com hello-webpage project showing the index.html file code

Show button on Glitch.com which allows you to preview a webpage in real-time whilst you're editing the code. Neat!

Common HTML Tags

Now you've probably already learnt a few new HTML tags (if you didn't cheat and skip the task hey?).

Here are some common ones:

<title>This is the page title. I go in the head part of the page**</title>**

<h1>Biggest Heading**</h1>**

<h6>Smallest Heading**</h6>**

<p>I **<i>**am**</i>** a ****paragraph of text**</p>**

<div>I am a generic block element used as a basic building block in HTML**</div>**

****I am a generic inline element****

<img src="dog.jpg" **alt**="A nice dog image here Google!" **/>**

<a href="about.html">Link to another page**</a>**

Remember, these tags should go into the **<body>** section of the webpage, not the **<head>** section.

Ready for your next practical?

Practical

Go ahead and implement some of these common tags into your webpage.

Again, if you're unsure about any of the tags or attributes which go into them, look them up on W3Schools.com/tags.

Advanced HTML Tags

Now that we've covered the basics, it's time to get a little bit more advanced.

If you're still having trouble reading the HTML code by this point, please go back and note down the *4 Language Rules of HTML* and keep them in front of you at all times. They will help you "**translate**" the code in your head from computer to human language.

Also, always keep the page W3Schools.com/tags open in a separate tab in your browser, as this is our **dictionary** to help understand HTML tags and their specific or generic attributes.

Pro tip: Let computers do the remembering of specific tags as they tend to be better at that, humans are very forgetful beings! Instead, just practice looking these tags up and learning how to use them.

The following sections all contain a **code snippet**, followed by a **practical exercise**.

How to add an image

Code Snippet

```html
<img src="" alt="This is a picture of a..." width="200">
```

Pro tip: Adding the *img* tag's specific *alt* attribute makes you a good citizen of the Internet, as this generally helps accessibility users to understand what this image is all about if they are using a text-only screen reader.

Notice we have also added an *img* specific *width* attribute which is measured in pixels.

One pixel is generally a single point or dot on the screen.

Practical
- Do a search for royalty free images of cats. Unsplash.com is a good source for this
- Here is one I've found earlier, but feel free to add one you like (usually you have to right-click the image and select *Copy image address* to get the image's link):
  https://unsplash.com/photos/gKXKBY-C-Dk/download?force=true&w=640
- Copy the code snippet to your webpage, replacing the *src* attribute's value with the image link of your choice
- Now, experiment with adding a *height* attribute
- Next, try removing the *width* attribute to see what happens. Exciting, hey?

How to add a bullet-point list

Let's be honest - lists are extremely important in conveying information.

So let's add one to your webpage.

Code Snippet

```html
<ul>
    <li>Apples</li>
    <li>Strawberries</li>
    <li>Grapes (seedless)</li>
</ul>
```

Practical
- Copy the code snippet to your webpage
- Modify the items in the list to your liking! Suggestion: add some items you need to buy on your next trip to the supermarket :)

How to add an audio

Adding a media element on a webpage is a bit more involved in terms of code, but once you know how to do it it's pretty straightforward!

Code Snippet

```html
<audio controls>
  <source src="" type="audio/mpeg">
  Your browser does not support the audio tag.
</audio>
```

Practical

- Do a search for royalty free MP3 music. FreeMusicArchive.org is a good source for this
- Copy the code snippet to your webpage, replacing the *source* tag's *src* attribute with the audio link of your choice (Make sure it ends in .mp3)
- Test the audio plays
- Feeling adventurous? Find out another *source type* that the audio tag supports, try to find one and add it to your page, replacing the existing one

How to add a video

The way to add videos can vary depending upon what the origin of the video is.

For example, for adding a video you have hosted somewhere and know the link to, there is a specific *video* tag you can use in HTML.

However, to use a video from a website like YouTube, they usually tend to provide all the code you need to embed the video into your website.

Code Snippet

```
<iframe width="200" height="200" src="" frameborder="0"
allow="accelerometer; autoplay; encrypted-media; gyroscope;
picture-in-picture" allowfullscreen></iframe>
```

Practical
- Do a search on YouTube.com for a video you like
- On YouTube, click the *Share* button, then the *Embed* button
- Copy and paste the code you are given to your webpage on Glitch.com
- If you're struggling to find a video, use the code snippet and add this funny cat video link https://www.youtube-nocookie.com/embed/XyNlqQId-nk to the *src* attribute
- Test the video plays

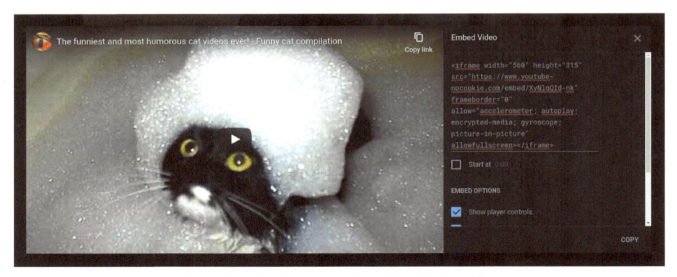

Embed code showing for a YouTube video

How to add a table of information

Code Snippet

```html
<table>
  <tbody>
    <tr>
      <th>Month</th>
      <th>Savings</th>
    </tr>
    <tr>
      <td>January</td>
      <td>$100</td>
    </tr>
  </tbody>
</table>
```

Practical
- Copy the code snippet to your webpage
- Modify it by adding at least **one column** and **one row** of your choice
- To the *tr* tag, add the *colspan* attribute with a number value. See the effect
- To the *tr* tag, add the *rowspan* attribute with a number value. See the effect
- Look up any tags you don't understand on W3Schools.com/tags

How to add internal & external links

Code Snippet

```html
<p>
  <a href="https://google.com">Click me!</a>
</p>

<p>
  <a href="about-us.html">Click me (goes to an internal page)!</a>
</p>
```

Practical
- Copy the code snippet to your webpage
- On Glitch.com, click the *New File* button to add an *about-us.html* file to your website (see image below for more information)
- Populate this new HTML file with the *Basic Structure of a HTML Page* that we covered in a previous chapter
- Test both links work as expected

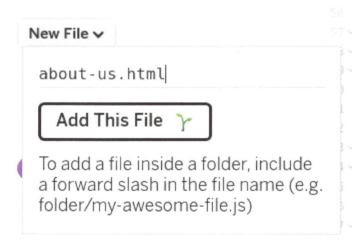

The New File option helps add a new HTML page to your website

How to create a form

The following example contains a lot of code, but don't let that scare you.

Always try to read the code one line at a time, and make sure you fully understand it.

In a real-world context we would never submit a form this way: by forcing the user to send an email manually via their default email program. However, without JavaScript, this is the best we can do for now.

Code Snippet for *index.html*

```html
<p>
   <a href="contact_me.html">Click me (goes to contact me form)!</a>
</p>
```

Code Snippet for *contact_me.html*

```html
<!DOCTYPE html>
<html lang="en">
<head>
   <title>Contact me</title>
   <meta charset="utf-8">
   <meta http-equiv="X-UA-Compatible" content="IE=edge">
   <meta name="viewport" content="width=device-width, initial-scale=1">
</head>
<body>
   <form action="mailto:me@example.com" method="get" enctype="text/plain">
     <p>Name: <input type="text" name="name" required></p>
     <p>Email: <input type="email" name="email" required></p>
     <p>
       Comments:
       <br />
       <textarea name="comments" rows="30" cols="50" required>Send your
comments to the website.</textarea>
       <br />
     </p>

     <p>
       <input type="submit" name="submit" value="Send">
       <input type="reset" name="reset" value="Clear Form">
     </p>
   </form>
</body>
```

```
</html>
```

Practical
- Create a new file *contact_me.html*
- Populate this with the [code snippet for *contact_me.html*](#)
- Add an internal link to this form from your index.html
- Update the *form* tag's *action* attribute to go to your email address
- Test both the internal link and form works by filling it in and clicking the *Send* button (it should open up your default email program and compose an email to you)
- Bonus Points: Look up some more form elements and add them to your form

Block vs Inline Elements

We've now covered quite a lot of practical, but it's back to a bit of theory for now!

An important concept to understand is that HTML elements come in two flavours:

- Block Elements - These **do not** let any other elements sit beside them e.g. **<div>**, **<p>**, **<ul>**, **<h1>** to **<h6>**
- Inline Elements - These **do** let other elements sit beside them e.g. **<span>**, **<a>**, **<img />**, **<label>**, **<input />**, **<i>**, **<strong>**

The easy way to understand this is if you think of a paragraph.

A paragraph needs to have space before and after it, otherwise it would not be a paragraph!

So this is why a paragraph is a block element.

However, what goes into a paragraph?

You may have text that is **bold** (**<strong>**), *italics* (**<i>**), contains some links (**<a>**) etc. so these tags need to form part of the paragraph and sit next to each other. This is why they are inline elements.

Practical
- Identify **two** other elements which are block elements. Add them to your webpage and see the effect
- Identify **two** other elements which are inline elements. Add them to your webpage and see the effect

---

How To Take A Sneak Peek At Any Website's Code

Now that your knowledge of HTML elements, tags and attributes is growing, the best way to further your learning is by taking a sneak peek under the hood of websites you visit–especially ones you like!

Most modern browsers contain a set of tools–called the *F12 Developer Tools*–which are usually used by developers to inspect, develop and test websites.

So how can you access these developer tools? There are a number of ways:

- Right-click your mouse anywhere on the webpage, and click the *Inspect* option
- Press the *Fn* key + *F12* combination on your keyboard
- Go into your browser's Options menu → More tools → Developer tools

F12 Developer Tools in Google Chrome with the Elements tab active

---

Practical
- Open the F12 Developer Tools on a website you like, and go to the *Elements* tab
- Use the "Select an element..." tool to pick an element on the screen and inspect its HTML

Share Your Website With The World

Now that you've built a fairly complex website, it's time to share it with the world.

Use the following option to find the link to your website:

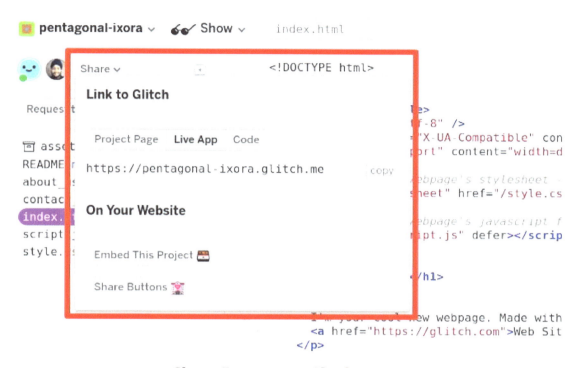

Share Buttons on Glitch.com

Getting feedback early and often is an important part of website development.

So be sure to ask for feedback and take any criticisms on board and use them to help improve your website further.

If you don't get a fully positive response to your website at this stage, it is understandable because we have not yet styled it with **CSS** or added interactivity with **JavaScript**.

Do look out for my upcoming books at <u>JasdeepKhalsa.com/books</u> where we'll build on this example to create a beautiful, functional website.

Summary

By now you're well on your way to becoming a HTML ninja.

You've already achieved so much, so take a moment to pat yourself on the back for making it this far!

In just one short hour we have learnt the basic rules of HTML, looked at everything from simple to advanced HTML tags and learnt how to use a code editor to make our website. We've also learnt how to take a sneak peek at the code behind any website we like.

HTML is an ever evolving language with a HUGE number of **elements**, **tags** & **attributes**, so be sure to keep on learning and exploring it throughout your life.

At the beginning of this book we aimed to be able to:

- Build a website from scratch
- Edit an existing website or HTML template

So how did we do?

Please do send me any feedback at JasdeepKhalsa.com/contact-us as we shall use this to further improve this book for everyone.

Well done once again, and keep on web developing!